BRANDYWINE CRITTERS

BRANDYWINE CRITTERS

Nature Crafts from "A Brandywine Christmas"

by volunteers of the Brandywine River Museum,
Brandywine Conservancy

Edited by Donna M. Gormel and Lucinda C. Laird

Photography by Michael Kahn

Good Books

Intercourse, PA 17534

Design by Dawn J. Ranck
Drawings on pages 6, 9, and 10 by Cheryl Benner
Cover photo in lower right corner by Mark Gormel
All other cover photos by Michael Kahn

BRANDYWINE CRITTERS: NATURE CRAFTS FROM "A BRANDYWINE CHRISTMAS"
Copyright © 1995 by Brandywine Conservancy, Inc.
Chadds Ford, PA 19317
International Standard Book Number: 1-56148-178-5
Library of Congress Catalog Card Number: 95-34637

Library of Congress Cataloging-in-Publication Data
Brandywine critters : nature crafts from "a Brandywine Christmas" / by
volunteers of the Brandywine Conservancy.
        p. cm.
    ISBN 1-56148-178-5
    1. Christmas decorations. 2. Nature craft. I. Brandywine
Conservancy.
TT900.C4B69   1995
745.594′ 12--dc20   95-34637
                                                              CIP

Table of Contents

Photograph by Mark Gormel

Introduction

Teasel, pokeweed, indigo, curly pea. These might be the ingredients of a magic potion or a wizard's brew, but they are not. Rather, they are the elements for one of the most enchanting holiday experiences in North America. These natural materials are among the components used to create the remarkable "critters" for which the Brandywine River Museum's annual holiday display, "A Brandywine Christmas," has gained renown.

Critters can be animals or angels. They are historical figures and storybook characters. They depict famous and infamous people. However, they are not the usual fare for a museum of American art. How, then, did they come to be at the Brandywine River Museum?

Early in the Brandywine River Museum's history, a group of volunteers was asked to decorate a small Christmas tree as part of "A Brandywine Christmas," the Museum's annual holiday display. To emphasize the Museum's role as part of the Brandywine Conservancy, which is dedicated to protecting the natural, cultural, and historical resources of the region, it was suggested that the tree be decorated with natural materials such as pods, seeds, grasses, and leaves. It was early November, and the holiday display was scheduled to open the day after Thanksgiving.

By necessity, the woods, fields, and roadsides of the Brandywine Valley became the volunteers' main resource. Those first ornaments were simple, unadorned pinecones, teasel pods, milkweed cases, and dried flowers.

Through the years, the critters have become more and more elaborate. Each year, a theme is chosen and thousands of critters are created to bring it to life. An Americana tree featured Betsy Ross stitching Old Glory, and the Statue of Liberty, holding her torch aloft. The Story Book tree was adorned with Cinderella, Big Bird and Babar, and Goldilocks and the Three Bears. Recently, a Musical tree inspired the creation of three "critter" tenors—Pavoratti, Carreras, and Domingo—along with critter choirs, orchestras, and instruments.

For each critter the basic ingredients are the same. It is the way the materials are put together that lends each critter its distinct character. Interesting shapes, colors, and textures are of primary importance.

Because critter construction is part of the Brandywine Conservancy, gathering plant materials is always done with conservation in mind. Plants are always cut, never pulled out by the roots. Seeds are shaken out of the seed head at the site, allowing future plants to germinate. Materials are carefully preserved and stored; what is not used one year is saved for the next.

In 1984 the volunteers' hard work and creativity paid off when they were invited to decorate the main Christmas tree in the Reagan White House. Because more than 3,000 ornaments were required for the project, many hours of preparation by both volunteers and museum personnel preceded the trip to Washington. Because the first lady—Nancy Reagan—loved red, many ornaments incorporating that color were created. Lots of cockscomb and euonymous was used!

The critters continue to be a source of joy each year for the volunteers and visitors alike. Through articles in national magazines, the critters have become known nationwide. It is a source of pride for both the Brandywine River Museum and the Brandywine Conservancy that these little creatures have become ambassadors for the mission of preserving the art and nature of the beautiful Brandywine River valley.

The Brandywine critters can be seen by visitors from late November through early January as part of the Brandywine River Museum's annual holiday display.

— Libby Dean and Anne Scarlett, Museum Volunteers

How to Collect
and Preserve Materials

Cornhusk

The Brandywine critters are made in the Museum's Critter Workshop, a large room set aside specifically for critter construction. It looks like many other craft workshops, with shelves loaded down by tubs of natural materials and all manner of dried flowers and pods hanging from the ceiling. The workshop officially opens each March, two months after the previous year's holiday display has been dismantled.

Mica

Approximately 35 volunteers have their first meeting and work gets underway in earnest. First comes the repair of critters from the "hospital box." Then the group begins preparing more than 7500 new critters for both the holiday display and the sale which benefits the Museum Volunteers' Art Purchase Fund. Material gathering goes on year round. (See calendar on page 8.)

Preparation of materials is important but not difficult. All organic material must be dried before it is used. Some materials, such as flowers and grasses, are hung and air dried. Others, such as the more delicate flowers, are dried in silica gel. Still others are dried in a slow oven for an hour or more and left in the oven until cool. Nuts, especially, must be oven dried to kill any worms or insects that might inhabit them. Pinecones with heavy sap may be placed in a slow oven (turned to lowest temperature) on cookie sheets covered with foil.

Pinecones

Calendar for Collecting Natural Materials

February
Weeping willow

March
Pussy willow

April
Pinecones

May
Cottonwood

June
Indian pipe
Peppergrass
Shepherd's purse
Wheat
Yarrow

July
Cattail
Dock
Figwort
Globe armaranth
Goat's beard
Redtop
Roses
Strawflowers
Teasel
Thistle

August
Acorns and caps
Artemisia
Black-eyed Susan
Campion
Celosia
Joe-pye-weed
Pearly Everlasting
Queen Anne's lace
Tansy
Teasel

September
Boneset
Evening primrose
Goldenrod
Osage orange
St. Johnswort
Spotted knapweed
Teasel
Velvet-leaf
Wormwood

October
Carrion-flower
Foxtail
Galls
Milkweed
Mullein
Rose hips
Statice
Vervain (blue)

Note: Gathering times will vary from region to region.

The sap "bakes" onto the pinecone, making it easier to handle and giving it a natural shine.

Teasel is one of the most often used components in Brandywine critters. It must be cleaned and its seeds must be removed. This can be done by gently rubbing together two pods with their points facing each other. Pods can also be cleaned with an old toothbrush. Because teasel is somewhat prickly and hard to handle, gloves should be worn.

Teasel

Milkweed pods provide wings, hair, fur, and tails for many critters. Pods are usually split while they are still green. Then the "fluff" inside is removed and the pod is propped open to dry.

Some green pods are peeled with a sharp knife slipped between the green skin and the inside of the pod. This leaves a lacy white shell which is perfect for angel wings.

Soybeans are dried and sprayed with either clear acrylic or spray adhesive to help keep them from splitting. Pokeweed

Milkweed
Pod

Soybean

seeds are obtained by crushing the pods and removing the seeds with tweezers. These are dried on sheets of wax paper. Mica must be washed, separated, and dried before it is ground. At the Critter Workshop, mica is ground a few layers at a time in an old blender. An old coffee grinder would work as well.

Cornhusks and other materials—okra, teasel, lunaria, and pinecones—can be bleached to remove mold and to lighten or remove color. Cornhusks are submerged in heavily diluted bleach (5 gallons water to 2 cups bleach) for one to three days depending on the amount of mold on the shucks. Husks are turned occasionally during bleaching to insure complete and even coverage. After bleaching, husks are removed from the solution, wrung out gently, and dried on a rack or old screen in bright sunshine. Rubber gloves should be worn at this step of the process to protect hands from the bleach.

Okra

Materials are always stored in paper bags or cardboard boxes to allow air to circulate and minimize mildew damage. If plastic containers are used, tops should be removed so that air can reach the materials.

Lunaria

Hot glue guns are used to construct critters because hot glue sets more quickly and holds more firmly to natural materials than other types of adhesives. Since hot glue has a tendency to drip or trail, it should be used carefully.

Construction of a few practice critters to become familiar with the materials is always a good idea. When critters are completed, they are sprayed with a clear acrylic to protect them and make them better able to resist breakage. Spraying must be done outside on a clear day. Never do the spraying indoors. Also never discard

Pokeweed Seed

leftover materials. Rather save them for another project.

The critters in this book are each marked with their level of difficulty. The majority of the projects are appropriate for beginning or intermediate levels. The few that are marked "advanced" require greater skill.

Critter construction takes little more than a hot glue gun, good dried materials, and an imagination. In the more than twenty years that Brandywine River Museum volunteers have been making critters, the designs have evolved from very simple figures to complicated tableaux. The only limit is the imagination!

—Roberta Domenick, Critter Workshop Chairperson

Christmas Critters

Every
Christmas season
the Brandywine River Museum
decorates trees
with "critters"—
imaginative characters
made from
natural grasses,
seeds, and pods.

Flying Angel

Materials:
1 acorn
30" of lightweight,
  green floral wire
cornhusk
beige thread
1 dried Clematis whorl
1 dried milkweed pod
assorted dried flowers
raffia

Equipment:
drill or sharp tool
glue gun
wire cutters
ruler
towel
white glue
hair clips
scissors
wax paper
clear acrylic spray

1. Using the point of the acorn for the nose, drill a small hole in the bottom of the acorn and fill with hot glue.

2. With wire cutters, cut a 6" length of floral wire and bend one end back on itself, about 1". Insert folded end of wire into the hole and hold until the glue is set. Put aside.

3. Soak cornhusk in hot water for ten minutes or until it is pliable. Spread the cornhusk on a wet towel to keep it damp while you are working.

4. For the arms, cut a 5" length of floral wire with wire cutters. From the dampened cornhusk, cut a 1½" x 5" rectangle. At the long side of the husk, place the wire at the edge and run a bead of white glue along the wire. Roll the husk tightly around the wire. With beige thread, tie tightly at the center of the rolled cornhusk. Place a hair clip on each end of the roll. Set aside and allow to dry overnight.

5. For the neck, cut a 1" x 3" piece of dampened cornhusk with scissors. Using white glue on one side of the strip, wrap tightly around the folded end of the wire extending from the acorn. This step is not visible in the finished critter; however, it is important for the formation of the body.

6. For the robe, cut two matching pieces of cornhusks in the shape of a large flower petal. These pieces should be 1" at the neck area, spreading to $3\frac{1}{2}$" at the bottom. The entire robe should be 5" in length.

7. To attach the gown to the head, place one cornhusk petal on wax paper. Coat one side of the petal with white glue. Place the acorn above the narrow end of the cornhusk petal with the 4" wire running down the center. Place the other cornhusk petal on top. Cover with a second piece of wax paper and press in place with a heavy object. Dry thoroughly overnight.

8. Remove from wax paper. Place the center of the arms on the front of the wired gown and glue into place.

9. For the bodice of the gown, cut two pieces of dampened cornhusk, 1" x 4" with scissors. Crisscross these pieces, one at a time, over the shoulder with the ends below the waist, in the front and back. Glue both strips into place and tie tightly with thread to form the waist.

10. With wire cutters, cut an 8" length of floral wire. Twist 1" of wire tightly around the neck, allowing 7" of wire for the hanger.

11. For the hair, glue the Clematis whorl to the acorn.

12. For wings, cut two 4" pieces of dampened cornhusk. These pieces should be a $\frac{1}{2}$" wide at the narrow end and gradually increase in width to $1\frac{1}{2}$" at the other end. With scissors, scallop the wide ends. See picture.

13. With wire cutters, cut two 3" lengths of floral wire. Glue the wire to the back of the wings.

14. To cover the wire in step 13, cut two 3" strips of cornhusk about a ½" wide. Cover one side of each cornhusk strip with white glue and glue into place over the wires. When dry, slightly bend the wings and glue the narrow ends behind the shoulders.

15. With scissors, cut the wide end off a milkweed pod. Glue assorted dried flowers into the remaining milkweed pod.

16. Bend the arms slightly to form the hands. Glue the milkweed pod to the hands. See picture.

17. To hide the wire hanger, glue small dried flowers at the angel's neckline.

18. At the waist, cover the thread with raffia and glue.

19. Spray with clear acrylic spray.

Cornhusk Angel

Materials:	**Equipment:**
cornhusk	towel
lightweight, green floral wire	ruler
beige thread	white glue
cotton ball	scissors
6" length of raffia	glue gun
lamb's wool	wire cutters
2 teasel bracts	paintbrush
ground mica	
4" teasel stem	
5 small, white dried flowers	

1. Soak the cornhusk for 10 minutes in hot water until pliable. While working with the cornhusks, spread them on a towel to keep them damp.

2. For the arms, cut a 7½" length of floral wire and a 1½" by 9" piece of cornhusk. Place the wire on the cornhusk and run a bead of white glue along the wire. Roll the husk tightly around the wire. After rolling, the cornhusk will extend ¾" beyond the wire at both ends. Fold the ¾" back on both sides and tie with beige thread. Using beige thread, tie at the center of the cornhusk roll.

3. For the sleeves, cut two 2" by 5" pieces of cornhusk. Wrap one piece loosely around one wrist, overlapping the wrist by ½", with most of the husk extending beyond the arm. Wrap and tie tightly at the wrist, gathering the fullness of the corn-husk into the tie. Fold the sleeve back toward the center, creating a puffed sleeve

at the wrist. Tie the opposite end of the sleeve tightly around the center of the arm. Repeat for the other sleeve.

4. For the head and chest, roll the cotton into a tight, 1" diameter ball. With scissors, cut a 4" by 6" piece of cornhusk. Place the cotton ball 3" down the length of the cornhusk at the edge. Holding the cotton ball in place, roll the husk lengthwise away from you. This will enclose the cotton ball in a cornhusk tube. With a firm grip on the head, twist one side of the husk as close to the head as possible. Fold the twisted husk back behind the head and tie all the husk tightly together just below the head to form the neck. The twist at the top of the head will be covered by the hair.

5. Just below the neck, separate the front and back husks and slide the arms between them, centering the arms beneath the head. Wrap the beige thread in a cross pattern, in the front and back, to secure the arms.

6. For the gown, cut two 5" by 9" pieces of cornhusk. Place one piece in the front and one in the back so they overlap 2" below the neck with most of the husk extending above the head. At the neck, wrap the beige thread around the husk and tie tightly. Fold down over the head. Cut two strips of cornhusk, ³/₄" by 5". Crisscross these strips over the shoulders, extending them below the waist in the front and the back. Tie tightly at the waist with raffia. With scissors, evenly trim the bottom of the gown.

7. For the hair use scissors to cut enough lamb's wool to cover the top and back of the head. Glue into place.

8. Paint the two teasel bracts with white glue and sprinkle with ground mica. Allow to dry thoroughly. Placing hot glue on the stem end of one bract, glue it onto the top of the head. With clippers, cut a 4" teasel stem and glue the other teasel bract to the top of the stem to make the wand. Insert and glue the end of the stem into the hand.

9. Cut an 8" length of lightweight, green floral wire and wrap 2" around the neck and twist tightly, leaving the remaining wire for the hanger.

10. For the wings, cut two pieces of cornhusk 2" by 6". Fold each piece in half, tying the cut ends of each strip tightly at the bottom. Using plenty of hot glue, attach the wings to the back of the body above the waist. To cover the ends of the wings, cut a 1¹/₂" by 2" piece of cornhusk. Fold to make a loop and glue the cut ends over the ends of the wings.

11. Glue small white flowers at the neckline to cover the hanging wire.

Santa Claus

Advanced

Materials:
1–5" pinecone
2–2" pinecones
2 large, long acorns
2 indigo seed pods for the boots
4–1½" pinecones
1 large English walnut
milkweed "silk" from
    the seed pod
bright red celosia
1 round, wooden toothpick
10 small hemlock cones
clear acrylic spray
assorted tiny dried flowers
    and seeds
½ of a dried milkweed pod
8" length of lightweight,
    green floral wire
2–4" by ¼" strips of wisteria pod
2 pinecone petals
1 teasel bract
1 pussy willow
1 tiny acorn
tiny twigs

birch or sycamore bark
½ of an outer casing of a buckeye
cotton

Equipment:
clippers
glue gun
drill
white glue
pointed scissors
wire cutters
aluminum foil

22

Santa's Body

1. With clippers, remove 1" of petals from the pointed end of a 5" cone.

2. With clippers, remove the pointed ends from the 2" pinecones.

3. Using a glue gun, glue the two 2" pinecones to the cut end of the 5" pinecone to form the upper legs of Santa. Be sure that all petals point down.

4. Glue the two large, long acorns to the base of the 2" pinecones. Remove the caps from the acorns.

5. For the shoes, glue the indigo seed pods to the acorns.

6. With a small drill bit, make a hole in the top center of the 5" pinecone. The head will be attached to this later.

7. For the arms, glue two of the 1½" pinecones together at a right angle. Repeat for the other arm.

8. With hot glue, attach the right arm flat against the body and extending forward. This arm will hold the wreath. Glue the left arm across the front of the body.

Santa's Head

1. Turn a large English walnut to select a ridge in the shell that resembles a nose and indentations on either side of the nose that resemble eyes. Drill a small hole in the bottom center of the walnut.

2. With white glue, attach strands of milkweed silk to the face of Santa, forming a beard, sideburns, mustache, and eyebrows. When dry, trim with sharp scissors to shape.

3. For the hat, glue celosia clippings to the top of the head. See picture.

4. Put a dab of hot glue into the drilled hole of the walnut and insert 1″ of a wooden toothpick.

5. Clip the extending end of the toothpick to ¼″, apply glue, and insert into the top center of the 5″ pinecone.

Wreath:

1. With hot glue, form a small 2″ wreath with hemlock cones.

2. Glue small flowers and seeds to one side of the wreath.

Santa's Bag:

1. Select half of a peeled milkweed pod that is 1″ by 4″ long. Cut a half circle from the top of the pod where the toys can be glued in.

2. With hot glue, attach milkweed pod to the back of the body.

3. Wrap 2″ of lightweight, green floral wire around the neck and twist tightly. Leave the remaining wire for the hanger.

4. Glue the two strips of wisteria pod from the left hand across each shoulder to the top corners of Santa's bag. These form the straps of Santa's bag.

5. For mittens, glue pinecone petals at the end of each arm.

6. Glue the wreath onto the right arm.

Santa's Toys:

1. Create a stuffed toy kitten by gluing a teasel bract tail to a pussy willow.

2. Make a tiny doll from an acorn, with the cap attached, by gluing onto a hemlock cone. Glue on small twigs for arms.

3. A toy airplane is made from crossed pieces of bark with wheels made from seeds.

4. For the sailboat, glue a thin piece of birch bark to a twig for the mast and insert into an outer casing of a buckeye.

5. Glue and arrange all of the toys into the top of Santa's pack. To fill in empty spaces, glue in dried flowers and seeds.

Final Trim:

1. Glue cotton around the edge of Santa's hat.

2. Glue cotton around the tops of the boots.

3. Add a pipe to Santa's mouth. Make the pipe from a twig and small seed. See picture.

4. Protect the face of Santa with aluminum foil to avoid turning the milkweed yellow. Spray the rest of Santa with clear acrylic spray.

Martynia Reindeer

Materials:
4 dried Martynia pods of
    similar size and color
1 small red seed
1 pussy willow
8" of lightweight,
    green floral wire

Equipment:
clippers
glue gun
wire cutters
clear acrylic spray

1. Select four dried Martynia pods of similar size and color. Cut off stems with clippers. Do not cut off prongs.

2. With clippers, remove prongs from one pod only. This pod will be used for the neck.

3. Use one pod for the head. Glue the neck pod to the head pod with the prongs curling forward. These prongs are the antlers. Hold until glue is set.

4. Using clippers, split a pod in half. Each half will have a prong. These will be the front legs.

5. Remove seeds from the split pod and save them for use in making other critters.

6. The remaining pod is used for the body and the hind legs with the prongs curling inward. Glue the split pod on either side of the body with the prongs curling inward. These prongs become the front legs. See picture.

7. Glue neck and head unit between the front legs. Hold until glue is set.

8. Glue dried red seed on the tip of the nose.

9. Glue pussy willow for tail.

10. Cut an 8″ length of lightweight, green floral wire with wire cutters.

11. For hanger, wrap 2″ of wire around the body at the base of the neck and twist tightly.

12. Spray thoroughly with clear acrylic spray.

Reindeer

Materials:
1 small teasel
1 large teasel
2 dried daylily stems
2 golden chain tree seeds
1 small dried red seed
2 white pinecone petals
4 soybeans
1 pussy willow
8" lightweight, green floral wire

Equipment:
clippers
pointed scissors
glue gun
wire cutters
clear acrylic spray

1. Using clippers, cut stem and bract from two teasels. The larger teasel will be used for the body, the smaller for the head.

2. With scissors, trim the smaller and larger teasels where the head and body join. The trimming enables a stronger bond when glued.

3. Using hot glue, glue the trimmed areas of the teasel together. Hold until glue is set.

4. For antlers, cut dried daylily stems to 1½". Use hot glue on ends of stems and insert into small teasel.

5. With points of scissors, make small holes in front of antlers for the eyes, glue in golden chain tree seeds using hot glue. Make a third hole for the nose and glue in red seed.

6. Trim white pinecone petals for ears, hot glue petals behind each antler, slightly to the outside of each daylily stem.

7. Using hot glue, glue in the four soybeans for legs. See picture for placement.

8. Using hot glue, glue in a pussy willow for the tail.

9. With wire cutters, cut an 8″ piece of lightweight, green floral wire. Wrap 2″ of wire once around body behind the neck and twist tightly. This is the hanger.

10. Spray entire critter with clear acrylic spray.

Lunaria Medallion

Materials:
1 teasel
8" length of lightweight,
   green floral wire
16 Lunaria petals
4–1½" pieces of German statice
1–1" diameter strawflower

Equipment:
clippers
pointed scissors
glue gun
tweezers
clear acrylic spray

1. Holding teasel by the stem, cut spikes from the bract with clippers.

2. With pointed scissors, cut a deep ¼" groove all around the teasel just above the bract.

3. For the hanger, wrap 2" of the wire into the groove and twist to secure.

4. With pointed scissors, cut another deep groove all around the teasel about ¼" above the first groove.

5. With clippers, cut off the top of the teasel ½" above the upper groove.

6. Trim the stem end of the Lunaria petals, but do not remove the outer points.

7. Glue the stem end of 8 Lunaria petals into the lower groove, slightly overlapping the petals as you work around the teasel. If possible, curl the petals upward.

8. Repeat step 7 in the upper groove using the remaining 8 Lunaria petals.

9. Glue pieces of German statice to the teasel at four equidistant places on the top of the Lunaria petals.

10. Glue the straw-flower on the top of the teasel. Hold in place until set.

11. With clippers, cut off the teasel stem close to the bract.

12. With tweezers, remove all glue threads.

13. Spray with clear acrylic spray.

Musical
Critters

The Musical tree—
a favorite
among Museum visitors—
inspires
the creation of
everything from
simple notes and instruments
to elaborate
choirs and orchestras.

Choir

Materials:
13 teasels of various lengths–
    4" and smaller
26 small white pinecone petals
    for beaks
26–1" white pinecone petals
    for wings
white birch tree bark
    for 12 choir books
26 golden chain tree seeds
2" twig for baton
26 very small pinecone petals
    for feet
piece of wide contorted willow
2–16" lengths of lightweight,
    green floral wire

Equipment:
pointed scissors
clippers
tweezers
glue gun
clear acrylic spray
wire cutters

1. DO NOT remove bracts or stems from teasels. With scissors, slightly trim bract spikes on all 13 teasels.

2. For beaks, with clippers or scissors, trim stem end of all small white pinecone petals to a slight point, approximately ³/₄" long.

3. For wings, with clippers or scissors, trim all 1" pinecone petals to ¹/₄" wide.

4. Cut white birch bark 1¹/₂" by 1" for 12 books. Soak them in warm water for 4–5 minutes to soften, then fold them in half lengthwise. (See picture.)

5. Using the largest teasel for the conductor, hold the teasel by the stem and cut tiny indentations for the eyes and beak with pointed scissors.

6. Using tweezers, glue two golden chain tree seeds in eye indentations.

7. For beak, glue two small white pinecone petals below and between the eyes. The pointed ends of the petals are glued into the teasel. See picture.

8. For the conductor's wings, cut small indentations below and slightly behind the eyes. Glue the white pinecone petals into the teasel with the right wing slightly higher than the left.

9. Glue the slender twig in the right wing of the conductor. Set aside.

10. For the choir, follow steps 6 and 7.

11. Attach wings to the 12 choir members with hot glue. Position them to hold the birch bark choir books.

12. Cut off the stems of teasels as close to the bract as possible. Glue two tiny pinecone petals for feet on each choir member and the conductor.

13. Arrange the choir on the contorted willow branch and glue each one in place. Hold each one until the glue is set.

14. Glue the conductor onto the willow facing the choir.

15. Secure the wire to each end of the choir branch.

16. With tweezers, remove all glue threads.

17. Spray the entire arrangement thoroughly with clear acrylic spray.

Musical Notes

Beginner

Materials:
1" diameter bamboo stem
3" straight, dried twig
8" length of lightweight,
    green floral wire
1 dried leaf
clear acrylic spray

Equipment:
small handsaw
clippers
medium-grade sandpaper
glue gun
wire cutters

1. Cut ¼" wide sections of the bamboo with a handsaw.

2. Cut straight, dried twigs to 3" lengths using clippers.

3. Sand the outside edges of bamboo rings with sandpaper.

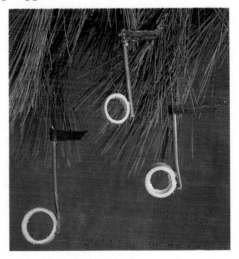

4. Glue a twig to one edge of a bamboo ring.

5. Cut wire to 8" length.

6. For the hanger, glue ½" of the wire to the twig and hold until set.

7. For the musical note's flag, cut a 1½" by ¼" strip of dried leaf. Glue the leaf around the twig and attached wire.

8. Spray with clear acrylic spray.

Musical Trio

Materials:
3–1½" teasels for the bodies
3–1" teasels for the heads
9 medium–sized golden chain tree
   seeds for eyes and nose
6 white pinecone petals for ears
2 pieces of a flat stem for the neck
   of the instruments
1–1¼" Paulownia pod for
   instrument
1 small piece of birch bark
1 small piece of cornhusk
1–1" Paulownia pod for instrument
2 small pinecone petals for the
   tops of instruments
6 pieces of strawflower stems for
   strings of the instruments

1 eucalyptus pod for the horn
1–2" long, thin twig
6 soybean pods for arms
6 tiny pinecone petals for feet
4 to 5" piece of pine bark mulch
3 grapevine curls for tails

Equipment:
clippers
pointed scissors
glue gun
knife
tweezers
clear acrylic spray

1. Holding the teasel by the stem, trim spikes from bracts of all teasels with clippers.

2. Cut off the long spikes from the tops of each teasel. On teasels to be used for heads, trim and taper teasel spikes with scissors to shape the face.

3. With glue gun, attach head and body teasels to form three critters. See picture for placement.

4. With clippers, remove bract from head teasels only.

5. With pointed scissors, cut tiny indentations in head teasels for eyes and nose. Glue in golden chain tree seeds.

6. For the ears, trim round end of white pinecone petals, as uniformly as possible, to a $3/8''$ width. With clippers, cut stem end to a $3/8''$ length and cut that end to a slight point.

7. With glue gun, attach ears with the pointed side into the teasel and place slightly behind the eyes.

8. For the instruments, attach a length of flat stem, 2 to 3" long, to the larger Paulownia pod with a glue gun. Glue a piece of birch bark or cornhusk to the flat, open side of the Paulownia pod. When dry, trim bark or cornhusk to the shape of the pod. Repeat for the smaller instrument. Glue a pinecone petal to create the top of each instrument. At the base of the Paulownia pod, glue a $1/2''$ piece of stem to attach strings. For strings, glue 3 strawflower stems on each instrument, from the pinecone petal to the $1/2''$ stem. For the horn, glue a eucalyptus pod to the end of a 2" twig. (See picture.)

9. For arms, position and hot glue soybean pods on teasel bodies. (See picture for placement of arms in relationship to the instruments.)

10. To attach Paulownia pod instruments, trim off some spikes of teasel, with scissors, in order to fit the instrument to the body. Glue instrument to body and arms. Hold until set.

11. For the horn, see picture for placement and glue into place.

12. With clippers, remove stems from body teasels. Glue tiny pinecone petals to bract for feet.

13. For the stand, carefully split a 4 to 5" piece of pine bark mulch horizontally with a knife.

14. Position musicians on bark and glue each one individually onto the bark, holding until set.

15. For tails, attach and glue grapevine curls to the back of critters. Position the tails so they can be seen from the front. (See picture.)

16. With tweezers, carefully remove all glue threads.

17. Spray with clear acrylic spray.

Animal
Critters

Many
Brandywine critters
find their way—
two by two—
to this
delightful rendition
of Noah's Ark.

Elephant

Materials:
2 dried milkweed pods
2 pumpkin seeds for eyes
2 golden chain tree seeds for
    pupils
1 large, long leaf pinecone for the
    body
4–2" long pinecones for the legs
1–1" pussy willow for the tail

2 dried stems from Martynia pods
    for tusks
1 small strawflower

Equipment:
glue gun
scissors
clear acrylic spray

1. Select a broad piece of dried milkweed pod for the face with the tip of the pod being the trunk.

2. For eyes, glue the pumpkin seeds to the milkweed pod. (See picture.) Hold until the glue is set.

3. For pupils, glue a golden chain tree seed to the center of each pumpkin seed. Hold until the glue is set.

4. For the ears, arrange two equal length milkweed pods on either side of the face and glue them to the face. The ears should slightly overlap the face and meet at the top.

5. Take the long leaf pinecone and position the face at the smaller, tapered end of the cone. Glue the face to the body and hold until set.

6. For the legs, select four 2" straight pinecones and glue into position. You must force the legs up into the pinecone body and hold until set.

7. For the tail, glue a large pussy willow in place.

8. For tusks, cut and glue curved pieces of dried Martynia stems between the ears and the trunk on either side of the face.

9. Glue a strawflower to the top of the head, where the ears and face meet.

10. Spray with clear acrylic spray.

Koala

Materials:
1 large teasel for body
1 medium teasel for head
2 small teasels for ears
2 golden chain tree seeds
1 watermelon seed
1-7" branch
4 soybeans
3" piece of pine bark
8" length of lightweight,
   green floral wire

Equipment:
clippers
glue gun
pointed scissors
tweezers
white glue
wire cutters
clear acrylic spray

1. With clippers, slightly trim all teasels.

2. For body, stand largest teasel upright and glue medium teasel to the top of the large teasel for the head.

3. For the ears, hot glue the small teasels towards the back of the medium teasel. See picture for placement.

4. Using pointed scissors, cut three small indentations for eyes and nose.

5. Using tweezers, pick up the golden chain tree seeds and glue them into place for eyes.

6. For the nose, glue watermelon seed into place.

7. Glue the koala to the base of the 7" branch.

8. For legs, glue soybeans to teasel and branch. (See picture for placement.)

9. Using white glue, glue the koala to the 3″ piece of pine bark. Hold until firm.

10. Wrap 2″ length of wire around the neck, twist tightly, allowing 6″ of wire for the hanger.

11. Spray with clear acrylic spray.

Lion

Materials:
2 teasels
3 golden chain tree seeds
small bunch of tan celosia
4 soybean pods
1 Clematis whorl
6 pine needles
8" length of lightweight,
    green floral wire

Equipment:
clippers
glue gun
pointed scissors
wire cutters
clear acrylic spray

1. With clippers, remove stem and bract from each teasel.

2. Shake seeds from teasel and discard seeds.

3. Trim sharp points of the teasel to make a smoother surface.

4. Using a glue gun, glue smaller teasel onto bract end of larger teasel. See picture.

5. For the eyes and nose, cut three small holes into the teasel head using pointed scissors. Glue in 3 golden chain tree seeds.

6. Trim stems from the tan celosia, leaving the flowers only.

7. For the lion's mane, glue small clumps of celosia on top of the teasel head and down the sides of the teasel. Gradually add celosia until you have the desired look.

8. Using pointed scissors, cut four small holes into the bottom of the teasel body for the legs.

9. For the legs, glue soybean pods into the holes cut in step 8.

10. Using a glue gun, glue Clematis whorl into the rear top of teasel body for the tail.

11. Using scissors, cut six pine needles approximately 1½" long.

12. Glue 3 pine needles on each side of the teasel near the nose for whiskers.

13. With wire cutters, cut an 8" length of lightweight, green floral wire.

14. For hanger, wrap wire once around the middle of the body and twist tightly.

15. Spray with clear acrylic spray.

Camel

Materials:

2 rhizome roots from a sandy
  shore plant: one small and
  one large, their shapes should
  suggest a head and body
1 small white bean half
2 pokeweed seeds
2 milkweed seeds
1 white pinecone petal
brown cornsilk
4–4" lengths of eucalyptus branch
4 beechnut hull halves
1–$1/8$" by $2^1/2$" strip cut from a
  sturdy, green leaf such as
  magnolia, not dried

1 yellow segment of bittersweet
  fruit capsule
1 red pepperberry
7" length of lightweight,
  green floral wire

Equipment:

glue gun
white glue
scissors
small container
clippers
wire cutters
needle nose pliers
clear acrylic spray

1. Position smaller rhizome root against larger one to form the head and body. Make sure that the hump is on top for the body. Glue into place.

2. Using the glue gun, glue the small white bean half to the face of the camel. (See picture for the placement.)

3. Apply a dab of white glue to the bean half. Position the two pokeweed seeds in glue for the eyes.

4. For the ears, glue a milkweed seed to each side of the camel's head at "ear level." (See picture.)

51

5. For the tail, attach a white pinecone petal in appropriate spot with glue.

6. Using scissors, cut the long strands of brown cornsilk into tiny lengths over a small container until there is about 3–4 tablespoons.

7. Run a bead of hot glue on top of the camel's head and down the back of the neck. Quickly sprinkle cornsilk trimmings over the hot glue for hair and mane. Repeat if needed for a fuller effect.

8. Run a bead of hot glue along the top of the camel's back and over hump. Include a dab of glue at the point of tail attachment. Again, quickly sprinkle corn silk trimmings over the glue for the hairy back effect and to cover the base of the tail.

9. Using the picture as a guide, glue four 4" lengths of eucalyptus to the underside of body for legs. Sprinkle trimmed cornsilk at sites of attachment to cover any excess glue before it cools.

10. At this stage, make sure all the legs of the camel appear equal in length. With clippers, trim so they are equal.

11. Glue a beechnut hull half to the bottom of each leg. The points of the hull should be facing forward. Before the glue cools, sprinkle attachment site with trimmed cornsilk to cover excess glue.

12. With scissors, cut a ⅛" by 2½" strip of sturdy, green leaf for the collar.

13. With one end of the strip, at the underside of the camel's neck, glue the collar around the neck ending at the original starting point.

14. For the bell, glue yellow bittersweet casing over the cut ends of the collar.

15. For the bell clapper, glue red pepperberry to the back bottom of the bittersweet casing. (See picture for placement.)

16. With wire cutters, cut a 7" length of lightweight, green floral wire.

17. For the hanger, twist one end of this wire around the tip of the needle nose pliers to form a small loop.

18. Decide where the hanging wire should go to balance the camel for hanging. Apply a good dab of hot glue to loop of wire and place loop in this spot. While holding in place, sprinkle on trimmed cornsilk to hide attachment site. Continue holding until glue hardens.

19. Spray entire ornament with clear acrylic spray.

Peanut Turtle

Materials:
1/2 *of large English walnut shell*
8″ of lightweight, green floral wire
5 whole peanuts
1 white pinecone petal
2 pokeberry seeds
1 Lunaria petal

Equipment:
electric or small manual hand drill
wire cutters
glue gun
wax paper
clippers
toothpick
white glue
clear acrylic spray

1. With drill, make a small hole through the center of a large English walnut shell half.

2. Using wire cutters, cut an 8″ piece of lightweight, green floral wire.

3. Insert 2″ of wire into drilled hole, bend and glue wire to the inside of walnut half using a glue gun. The remaining wire will be used to hang the turtle. Set walnut aside.

4. On wax paper, arrange four peanuts in a star formation with all four peanuts coming together in the center. Using a glue gun, glue them together at the center point. These will be the legs. Hold until the glue is set.

5. Using a glue gun, put glue on the underside rim of the walnut shell and center the shell on the top of the four peanuts. The narrow end of the walnut shell will be the back of the turtle. Hold until glue is firm.

6. Using the remaining peanut, glue between the front two peanuts and under the walnut shell to form the head. This peanut should be standing on end.

7. Use clippers to cut the white pinecone petal into a sharp point for the tail. Glue into place under the narrow portion of the walnut shell.

8. Using a toothpick, put a spot of white glue on each side of head. On wax paper, lay out two pokeberry seeds, wet finger and pick up one seed and place on spot of white glue, repeat with other seed.

9. Using a glue gun, glue one Lunaria petal to the underside of the turtle's body.

10. Allow white glue to dry thoroughly before spraying entire critter with clear acrylic spray.

Owl

Materials:
2–³⁄₄" matching acorn caps
1–3" spruce cone or teasel
1 beechnut hull
2–1" white pinecone petals
2–³⁄₄" white pinecone petals
1 long acorn or lima bean
8" length of lightweight,
      green floral wire

Equipment:
clippers
glue gun
tweezers
wire cutters
clear acrylic spray

1. Trim stems from acorn caps.

2. Glue acorn caps $\frac{1}{2}''$ from the top of spruce cone or teasel. Hold until set.

3. With clippers, cut beechnut hull into four points and glue one point above each acorn cap for ears.

4. For wings, glue large pinecone petals below and a little behind the eyes.

5. To make the feet, trim the pointed end of the spruce cone flat and glue smaller pinecone petals in place. Hold until set.

6. For the beak, glue long acorn or lima bean below acorn caps.

7. Wrap one end of wire around the body below the eyes and beak. Twist wire together to secure. Allow 5″ of wire for the hanger.

8. With tweezers remove all glue threads.

9. Spray thoroughly with clear acrylic spray.

Poodle

Materials:
8–1¹/₂" gumballs
3–¹/₂" gumballs
3 large golden chain tree seeds
1 beechnut hull
10" length of lightweight,
    green floral wire
10" length of raffia or grass
1 small dried flower

Equipment:
clippers
glue gun
tweezers
wire cutters
clear acrylic spray

1. Using clippers, trim off stems from all gumballs.

2. For muzzle, cut one small gumball in half with clippers.

3. With a small amount of glue, attach muzzle to one large gumball to make the head.

4. Glue one golden chain tree seed in the center of the muzzle for the nose.

5. For the ears, split the beechnut hull into four sections and glue the blunt end of a section into the gumball over and a little behind each eye.

6. For the top knot, glue a small gumball on top of the head and set aside.

7. For the body, using a small amount of glue, attach three large gumballs in a row. Hold them until set.

8. For the feet, glue four large gumballs under the body. (See picture for placement.)

9. Glue head on one end of the body. Hold carefully until set.

10. Glue one small gumball at the other end of the body for the tail.

11. Wrap one end of the wire around the first gumball of the body and twist together to secure. Leave 6″ of wire for the hanger.

12. Tie raffia or grass around the neck in a bow. Trim ends if they are too long.

13. Glue dried flower on top of head.

14. With tweezers remove all glue threads.

15. Spray heavily with clear acrylic spray.

Cat

Materials:
1 large hairy acorn
1 medium acorn cap
8" length of lightweight,
    green floral wire
2" twig
2 pokeberry seeds
4 pussy willows
3" length of foxtail
4–1" strawflower stems for
    whiskers

3" piece of pine bark
1 small acorn

Equipment:
clippers
glue gun
white glue
clear acrylic spray

1. Using clippers, trim excess curls from hairy acorn.

2. For the head, glue acorn cap to the hairy acorn and hold until firm.

3. Twist 2" of lightweight, green floral wire around the top section of the 2" twig. Glue the twig, with the wire attached, to the back of the body and head of the cat. This will act as a support for the body. This step is not visible in the picture.

4. For the eyes, white glue the pokeberry seeds into place.

5. For the ears and paws, glue pussy willows into place.

6. Glue foxtail into place for tail.

7. For whiskers, cut strawflower stems to 1" lengths and glue into place.

8. Glue completed cat onto 3″ piece of pine bark.

9. Glue acorn to pine bark piece.

10. Spray with acrylic spray.

Teasel Pig

Materials:
1 teasel
1 immature acorn
2 whole black peppercorns
1 beechnut hull
1 grapevine curl
4 small soybeans
8" lightweight, green floral wire

Equipment:
clippers
pointed scissors
glue gun
white glue
wire cutters
clear acrylic spray

1. With clippers, cut bract and stem from teasel.

2. Using pointed scissors, make small hole in narrow end of teasel opposite the end from which the stem and bract were removed. Glue the stem end of the immature acorn into the hole for the nose. Hold in place until set.

3. For eyes, cut two small holes above acorn with scissors. Glue in whole black peppercorns for eyes.

4. Using clippers, cut beechnut hull into four sections. Glue in one beechnut hull behind each peppercorn eye, having the pointed end being the tip of the ear. Save the other hulls for use in making additional critters.

5. With clippers, cut grapevine curl to approximately 1" and glue into place for tail.

6. Using hot glue, insert stem end of 4 soybeans for legs.

7. With wire cutters, cut 8″ length of lightweight, green floral wire. Wrap 2″ of wire around pig just behind the ears and twist tightly.

8. Spray with clear acrylic spray.

Playful
Critters

The Brandywine
River Museum
and the
Brandywine Conservancy
celebrate and preserve
the
rich natural history
of the
surrounding
river valley.

Ballerina Bear

Materials:
3–3" teasels
3–2" teasels
2–1" teasels
8" length of lightweight,
  green floral wire
3 golden chain tree seeds
4–1" pinecone petals
1 dried, red chili pepper
18" of raffia
4 lengths of cornhusk
6 eucalyptus leaves
3 small dried flowers

Equipment:
clippers
sharp pointed scissors
glue gun
tweezers
ruler
paper towels
needle
beige thread
wire cutters
clear acrylic spray

1. With clippers, remove the stem and bract from all teasels. Trim ¼" off the pointed tops of all the teasels.

2. For the legs, with pointed scissors, trim two of the 3" teasels where they will be joined with the other 3" teasel which is being used for the body. The trimming enables a stronger bond when glued. Hold in place until the glue has set.

3. For the arms, repeat the same technique in trimming as in step 2 using the 2" teasels. Glue the arms as close to the top of the body teasel as possible. See picture.

4. Using the 8" length of floral wire, make a 1" circle at one end, twist and place it on top of the body teasel. For the head, glue a 2" teasel on top of the body teasel and wire. The additional 7" of wire will be the hanger.

5. For the ears, glue the 1″ teasels in place. Hold until set.

6. For the eyes and nose, glue the 3 golden chain tree seeds in place, using tweezers.

7. For the hands, glue 1″ pinecone petals in the tips of the arms. The petals should be facing downward.

8. For the feet, glue pieces of dried, red chili pepper onto the 1″ pinecone petals. Trim the pepper to the exact shape of the petals. Tie two bows using $\frac{1}{8}$″ by 2″ lengths of raffia. Glue them to the red shoes. Glue the red shoes into the leg teasels. (See picture.)

9. With pointed scissors, cut a $\frac{1}{4}$″ ridge around the middle of the body for the location of the skirt. To determine the amount of cornhusk for the skirt, measure the waist.

10. For the skirt, using scissors, cut a 2″ wide by 12″ long piece of cornhusk. Soak the cornhusk for ten minutes, to make it pliable. After soaking, remove the excess water with paper towels. With needle and thread, carefully shirr cornhusk strip, to fit around the waist and to overlap $\frac{1}{4}$″ in the back. Apply glue in 1″ sections around the waist and push in cornhusk as you go. Do small sections at a time because the glue dries quickly.

11. From raffia, make a $\frac{1}{2}$″ wide by 6″ long braid. Glue braid around the waist, criss-crossing it in the front and letting the ends extend to the sides. Glue eucalyptus leaves and dried flowers on the ends of the braid. (See picture.)

12. Glue eucalyptus leaves and a small dried flower on the top of one ear.

13. Spray entire ornament with clear acrylic spray.

Raccoon Wreath

Intermediate

Materials:
4' of green, wild honeysuckle vine
12" of lightweight, green floral
    wire
1 large white pinecone
13 sprigs of dried rhododendron
    florets
1 tiny acorn
1 hickory nutshell
2 small hemlock cones
1 sweet gumball
2 medium teasels
4 Japanese holly seeds for eyes
4 matched, medium white
    pinecone petals for ears
2 matched, large white pinecone
    petals for tails

Equipment:
4 pinch-style clothes pins
hand or band saw
glue gun
clippers
wire cutters
clear acrylic spray

1. Remove all leaves from the honeysuckle vine. Twist vine into a 5" diameter wreath and secure with four pinch-style clothes pins.

2. Place the wreath in a 250° oven for approximately 20 minutes. If the vines are green, more time for drying may be required.

3. When the wreath is dry, remove clothes pins and wrap wreath sparingly with wire to keep wreath circular. Leave 4" of wire for the hanger.

70

4. With saw, slice 1" off the bottom of large white pinecone. Glue the sliced bottom piece to the top of the wreath.

5. Glue rhododendron florets to each side of the sawed pine cone on the wreath.

6. Glue tiny acorn to the center of the sawed pinecone.

7. Glue one section of the hickory nutshell to one side of the sawed pinecone and another section to the other side. See picture.

8. Glue one hemlock cone next to the hickory nutshell and repeat on the other side of the wreath.

9. With a saw, slice a gumball in half and glue to the wreath next to the hemlock cones.

10. With clippers, cut stems and bracts from teasels.

11. Glue teasels to the inside bottom of the wreath. The raccoons will appear to be swinging.

12. Glue Japanese holly seeds in place for eyes.

13. Glue four small pinecone petals for ears.

14. Glue two large pinecone petals for tails.

15. Spray thoroughly with clear acrylic spray.

Duck in Eggshell

Materials:
½ of brown or white eggshell
   (broken around the middle)
2 teasels (one small; one medium)
2 black seeds
5 white pinecone petals
8" of lightweight, green floral wire

Equipment:
small paintbrush
white glue
clippers
pointed scissors
glue gun
wire cutters
clear acrylic spray

1. Break eggshell around middle. Wash shell with soap and water, rinse and dry well.

2. Paint inside of shell with several coats of white glue (this will strengthen the eggshell).

3. Using clippers, cut bract from stem end of each teasel.

4. With pointed scissors, trim smaller and larger teasel where the head and body join. The trimming enables a stronger bond when glued. (See picture.)

5. Hot glue head to body using the smaller teasel for the head and the larger for the body. The stem end of the larger teasel should be facing outward to form the breast of the duck. Hold until glue is set.

6. Using the points of the scissors, cut a small hole in each side of the teasel being used for the head. Glue black seeds into these holes for eyes.

7. Using clippers, cut ends off pinecone petals for beak, wings and tail feather. Using the picture as a guide, glue pinecone petals into place using a hot glue gun.

8. Place a generous amount of glue in the inside of the eggshell, insert completed duck into eggshell and hold until firm.

9. With wire cutters, cut 8″ length of lightweight, green floral wire. Wrap 2″ of wire around neck of duck and twist tightly. This is the hanger.

10. Spray with clear acrylic spray.

Character Critters

Brandywine critters
sometimes
take on
storybook dimensions.
Visitors may encounter
"The Old Woman
in the Shoe"
or
"Goldilocks and the
Three Bears."

Baby Buggy

Beginner

Materials:
1 teasel
3 golden chain tree seeds
4 white pinecone petals
1 small dried flower
2 matched large acorn caps
$^1/_2$ of large English walnut shell
$4^1/_2$" green twig
8" length of lightweight,
   green floral wire

Equipment:
clippers
pointed scissors
glue gun
medium-grade sandpaper
wire cutters
clear acrylic spray

1. With clippers, remove stem and bract from teasel.

2. Using pointed scissors, cut three small holes into teasel for eyes and nose.

3. Using glue gun, glue 3 golden chain tree seeds for eyes and nose, using the holes that were cut in step 2.

4. With clippers, trim 4 white pinecone petals for arms and ears. Glue into place, using picture as a guide.

5. For hat, glue any small dried flower on top of teasel.

6. Remove stems from acorn caps using clippers.

7. For buggy wheels, lightly sand stem end of acorn caps to help hot glue adhere to sides of walnut shell. Glue each acorn cap on opposite sides of walnut shell.

8. Bend and glue green twig to the inside of walnut shell for buggy handle. Use a generous amount of glue in this step and hold until glue is hardened.

9. Apply ample amount of glue to base of critter, insert critter into walnut shell, and hold until set.

10. With wire cutters, cut an 8″ length of lightweight, green floral wire.

11. For hanger, wrap wire once around body just above walnut shell and twist tightly.

12. Spray entire ornament with clear acrylic spray.

Canoe

Materials:
1 small teasel
$^1/_2$ of a trumpet vine pod
1 small acorn
2 matched soybeans
$3^1/_2$" teasel stem
$^1/_2$ of a pistachio shell
4 dried corn kernels
a few dried flowers
8" length of lightweight,
   green floral wire

Equipment:
clippers
wire cutters
glue gun
clear acrylic spray

1. With clippers, remove stem and bract from teasel.

2. Hot glue teasel inside the center of the trumpet vine. Hold until set.

3. For the head, glue small acorn on top of teasel.

4. For the arms, glue matching soybean pods onto either side of the teasel. Hold until set.

5. For paddle, glue teasel stem onto left soybean pod.

6. Glue pistachio shell onto the end of the teasel stem.

7. Glue dried corn kernels into the back end of the trumpet vine pod.

8. Glue dried flowers into the front end of the trumpet vine pod and at the neck of the canoeist.

9. For hanger, wrap 8″ length of lightweight, green floral wire once around the body, just below the soybean arms.

10. Spray entire ornament with clear acrylic spray.

Golfer

Materials:
1–4" pinecone
4–2¹⁄₂" pinecones
1 acorn with cap
2" length of cornhusk
small amount of dried, red celosia
1–3" stick
2 watermelon seeds
1 dried, round, white bean for
   golf ball
2 Paulownia seeds

2 pokeberry seeds
9" length of lightweight,
   green floral wire

Equipment:
clippers
glue gun
scissors
white glue
wire cutters
clear acrylic spray

1. With clippers, slightly trim the sides of the pointed end of the large pinecone. This will enable the smaller pinecones to bond with the larger pinecone when glued.

2. For legs, glue pinecones to trimmed area of the larger pinecone. Hold firmly until set.

3. Repeat step 1 at the stem end of the large pinecone, for the placement of the arms. For arms, glue the stem ends of the pinecones to the top of the large cone. Curve the pinecones so the ends touch. See picture.

4. For head, glue acorn with cap to the top of the pinecone.

5. With scissors, cut a 2" length of cornhusk to ¹⁄₄" width. Using a glue gun, apply a small amount of glue around the neck. Wrap cornhusk around the neck and criss-cross in the front.

6. Glue small pieces of red celosia on the top of the acorn cap and around the neck.

7. For the club, apply glue to the tips of the arms and insert the 3" stick. Hold until set.

8. For the club head, glue the watermelon seeds to sides of the stick, at the bottom. For the ball, glue white bean to the inside of the club head. (See picture.)

9. Using clippers, trim the bottom of the pinecone legs so they are flat. For feet, glue Paulownia seeds on the bottom of the cones.

10. For eyes, apply a small amount of white glue to the acorn. Dampen your finger to pick up the pokeberry seeds and place the seed on the glue.

11. Wrap 3" of wire around the body and twist tightly, allowing 6" of wire for the hanger.

12. Spray with clear acrylic spray.

Pinecone Skier

Materials:
1–5" dried Catalpa pod
1–3" pinecone
1 hickory nut
8" length of lightweight,
    green floral wire
3" length of lamb's wool by
    1" wide
2 dried seed heads of black-eyed
    Susan flowers
2 soybeans
2 pussy willows
2–3" dried twigs
2 dried poppy pod tops

Equipment:
razor knife
clippers
glue gun
wire cutters
scissors
sharp pointed tool
clear acrylic spray

1. For skis, split Catalpa pod lengthwise with a razor knife. Cut the split pod to 5" lengths with clippers.

2. Glue the bottom of the pinecone to the center of the skis. Hold until firm.

3. Using clippers, cut top center pinecone petal from pinecone.

4. For the head, glue the hickory nut to the top center of the pinecone.

5. For the hanger, cut an 8" length of lightweight, green floral wire. Wrap 2" of the wire around pinecone slightly under the head and twist tightly.

6. For the hat, glue the lamb's wool to the hickory nut by placing a circle of glue on back half of the nut. Press wool into place with the seam in the back.

7. For the ear muffs, glue the dried black-eyed Susan centers below the lamb's wool.

8. For arms, insert and glue the stem end of the soybeans into the pinecone.

9. For mittens, glue pussy willows to the ends of soybeans.

10. For the ski poles, cut two 3" dried twigs.

11. With razor knife remove tops from the dried poppy pods.

12. Using any sharp pointed tool, make a hole in the center of the two poppy pod tops.

13. Insert twigs into holes with bottom of twigs extending $\frac{1}{2}$" beyond poppy pods.

14. Glue the poles to the inside of the pussy willows approximately $\frac{1}{4}$" above the mittens.

15. Spray with clear acrylic spray.

Goldilocks and the Three Bears

*Note: Due to the degree of difficulty in making this ornament,
the materials and instructions are divided into sections.*

Materials for Goldilocks:
dried gall for head
4" teasel
6–5" by 1" pieces of cornhusk
2 dried soybean pods
dried Clematis whorls for hair
6 strawflowers
dried goldenrod
3" slice of thin wood or flat bark
5 poplar seed petals

Equipment:
clippers
awl
glue gun
mister
scissors
wax paper
wire cutters
clear acrylic spray

1. Using clippers, cut stem from one end of gall.

2. Using clippers, cut stem and bract from 4" teasel. With awl, make a hole in the stem end of the teasel.

3. For the head, glue gall stem into the teasel hole.

4. Dampen cornhusk with a mister.

5. For the gown, glue the six pieces of cornhusk to the teasel body, overlapping as you work.

6. Glue the soybean arms in place.

7. Carefully hot glue the Clematis whorls to the top of the gall head.

8. Glue the strawflowers and dried goldenrod on the gown and around the neck.

9. Glue Goldilocks to 3" base. Hold until set.

10. Glue the five poplar seed petals to the base. See picture for placement.

Materials for Bears:

18–teasels of varying sizes
6 golden chain tree seeds
6 pinecone petals
12 squash seeds

3 immature acorns for noses
3 acorn caps
dried corn kernels for bowls

1. With clippers, cut stems and bracts from all teasels. Trim all teasels severely with sharp scissors.

2. With scissors, cut indentations where the legs and arms join the teasel body. This will enable a stronger bond when glued.

3. When making the three bears, use the various sizes of teasel to create one large, one medium and one small bear.

4. Glue head, arms and legs to body teasels. Hold until set.

5. For eyes, glue in golden chain tree seeds.

6. For ears, trim pinecone petals with scissors and glue in place.

7. For paws, trim squash seeds to fit the bottom of the paws and glue in place.

8. For noses, glue immature acorn caps to the tips of teasels.

9. Fill the acorn caps with glue, and press dried corn kernels into bowls.

10. Glue the bowls between the front paws and under the heads of bears. Hold until set.

Materials for House:

6–4" lengths of straight, thin branches
6–6" lengths of straight, thin branches
6–7" lengths of straight, thin branches
8" length of lightweight, green floral wire

5" piece of dried celosia stem
2–2" pieces of dried celosia stems
1–4" by 1½" strip of lightweight bark
6 pieces of white statice
1 strawflower

1. With clippers, cut the straight, thin branches to the lengths listed above.

2. On wax paper, lay out the house design. Use the 7" lengths for the bottom and the ceiling rafters, the 6" lengths for the sides and the 4" lengths for the roof. There should be three branches per section.

3. When design is complete, start gluing at the corners. Hold until the glue is set.

4. With wire cutters, cut an 8" length of lightweight, green floral wire. Twist tightly around the branches at the peak of the roof for hanging.

5. For the bench, cut a 5″ piece of dried celosia stem for the bench top and two 2″ lengths for the bench legs. Glue the legs to the base of the house and hold until set. Glue bench top to legs.

6. Glue Golidlocks to the side of the house.

7. Glue the bears to the bench. The largest bear should also be glued to the side of the house.

8. Glue 4″ by 1¹/₂″ strip of bark to the front bottom of the house.

9. Decorate the house by gluing statice to the top and corners of the house. Glue a strawflower to the peak of the house.

10. Spray with clear acrylic spray.

How to Remedy Mistakes

Don't panic and don't despair. Some of the best critters are made from mistakes.

If you wish to change your creation, a simple remedy would be to soften the glue with a handheld hair dryer. Use the dryer on the lowest setting for several minutes or until the glue is pliable. You should now be able to separate the materials and remove any excess glue before starting over.

At this point, let your creativity take over.

About the Volunteers

Libby Dean and **Anne Scarlett** have been involved with the Brandywine River Museum since it opened in 1971. They have volunteered in a multitude of capacities, serving as docents, creating masterful flower arrangements, and supporting the volunteers' annual fund raising efforts, including the Antiques Show and Critter Sale. They created the first critters in 1973 and have helped to bring national recognition to the Brandywine River Museum and its annual holiday display.

Roberta Domenick has volunteered for the Brandywine River Museum since 1984. Her expertise is critters. She has served as chairperson of the Critter Workshop for six years, shepherding the program to its present level of excellence and creating thousands of critters herself. Bert's husband, **Ben,** is equally involved in the Critter Workshop.

Other volunteers currently in the critter program: Grace Barrington, Kitty Benton, Jeanne Bicking (1995 workshop assistant chairperson), Ellen Craney, Bette Daller, Jack Daller, Dotty Dalrymple, Marie Dalton, Doris Dengler, Ginger Doran, Olga Fischer, Mary Lou Hale, Jo Harpham, Penny Hirannet, Naomi Hirano, Christine Hodapp, Evelyn Hopkins, Adrienne Karr, Basil Kershner, Helen Kershner, June Libbey, Ruth Lieberman, Lorraine Mostyn, Yachai McCarthy, Jan McClelland, Pat McGrail, Jim Michell, Donna Neithammer, Norma Nelson, Anna Marie Newman, Sandra Pacitti, Marjorie Payne, Dorothy Plank, Joanna Savery, Maggie Scott, Estelle Sherman, Eva Shultis, Shirley Stowe, Evie Strawbridge, Lilian Sundet, Connie Swensson, Alice Taylor, Nance Tieste, and Jeanette Webber.

About the Editors

Donna M. Gormel is Coordinator of Volunteers for the Brandywine Conservancy and its Brandywine River Museum. She has been with the Conservancy since 1982 and presently manages a volunteer force of more than 200 people.

Lucinda C. Laird is Director of Public Relations for the Brandywine Conservancy and its Brandywine River Museum. She has directed publications, media relations, and special events for the Conservancy since 1990. She is the author of *American Elegance* (New York, Abbeville Press, 1988).

About the Photographer

Michael Kahn has contributed photographs to many magazines, newspapers, and other publications. A book of his photographs, *Brandywine,* was published in 1990 by Jared Press (Wilmington, DE). His work has been exhibited at several museums and galleries, including the Butler Institute of American Art in Youngstown, Ohio. His current projects include books on Pennsylvania and Maine.

About the Brandywine River Museum

Founded in 1971, the **Brandywine River Museum**'s American art collections include the foremost collection of art by members of the Wyeth family, including N.C., Andrew, and Jamie Wyeth. The Museum also features renowned collections of American illustration and landscape and still life painting. Located in a restored, mid-19th century grist mill on the banks of the Brandywine River amidst gardens featuring wildflowers and native plants, the Museum is a pleasure in any season. It is particularly charming each year at Christmas, when its remarkable collections are accented by the volunteers' critters, angels, and stars.